EASY PIANO

BILLIE EILISH
DONT SMILE AT ME

ISBN 978-1-5400-7039-5

For all works contained herein:
Unauthorized copying, arranging, adapting, recording, Internet posting, public performance,
or other distribution of the music in this publication is an infringement of copyright.
Infringers are liable under the law.

Visit Hal Leonard Online at
www.halleonard.com

Contact us:
Hal Leonard
7777 West Bluemound Road
Milwaukee, WI 53213
Email: info@halleonard.com

In Europe, contact:
Hal Leonard Europe Limited
42 Wigmore Street
Marylebone, London, W1U 2RN
Email: info@halleonardeurope.com

In Australia, contact:
Hal Leonard Australia Pty. Ltd.
4 Lentara Court
Cheltenham, Victoria, 3192 Australia
Email: info@halleonard.com.au

COPYCAT

Words and Music by BILLIE EILISH
and FINNEAS O'CONNELL

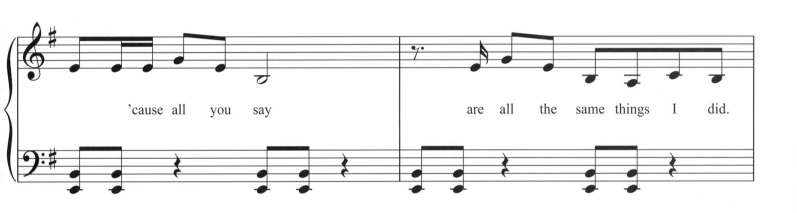

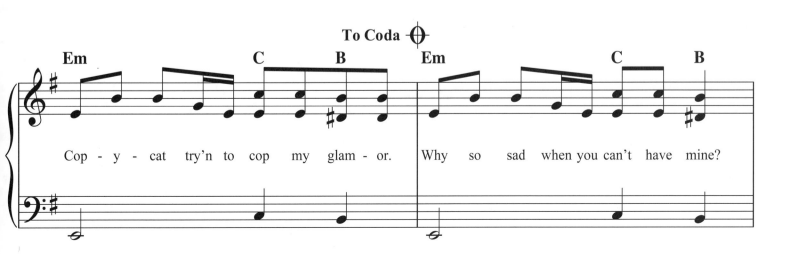

N.C.

Call me cal-loused, call me cold.

You're i - tal - ic, I'm in bold. _____ Call me cock - y, watch your tone. You bet - ter

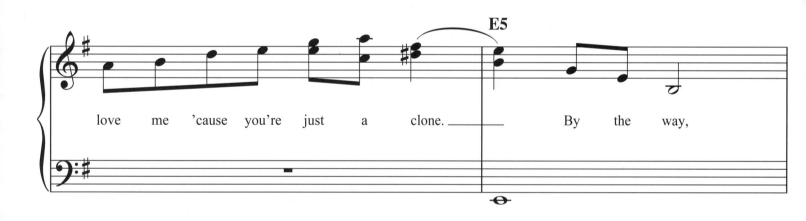

E5

love me 'cause you're just a clone. _____ By the way,

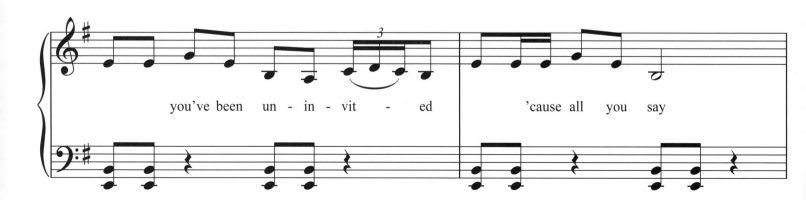

you've been un - in - vit - ed 'cause all you say

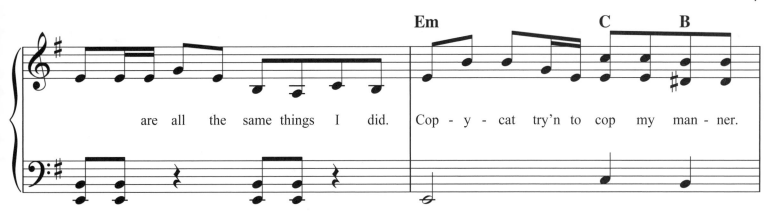

are all the same things I did. Cop - y - cat try'n to cop my man - ner.

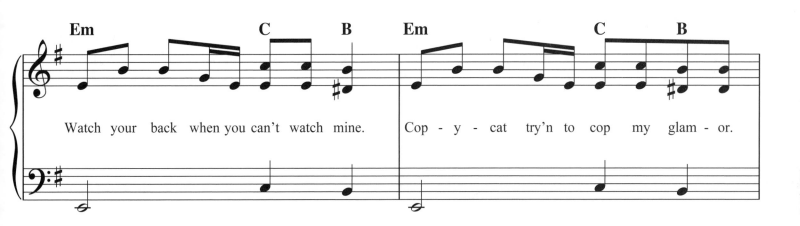

Watch your back when you can't watch mine. Cop - y - cat try'n to cop my glam - or.

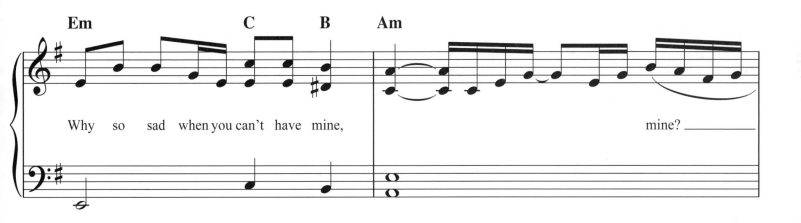

Why so sad when you can't have mine, mine? _____

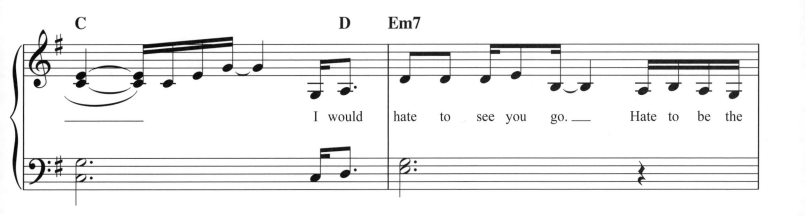

_____ I would hate to see you go. ___ Hate to be the

8

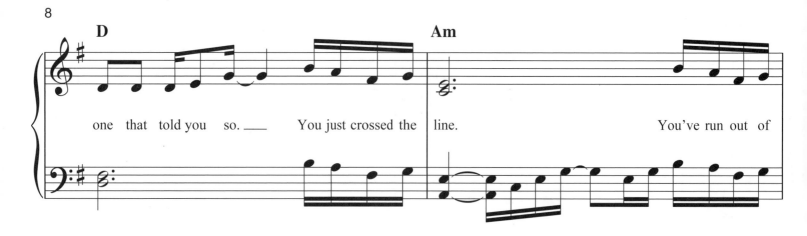

one that told you   so.___   You just crossed the   line.   You've run out of

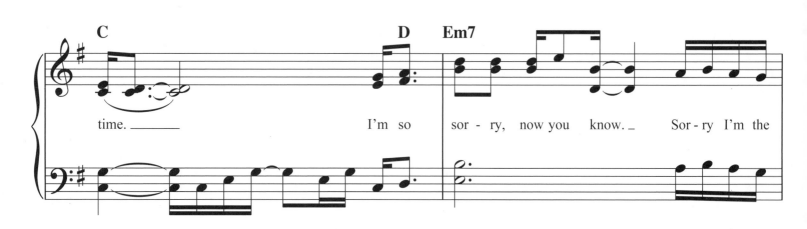

time. _____   I'm so   sor - ry, now you   know._   Sor - ry I'm the

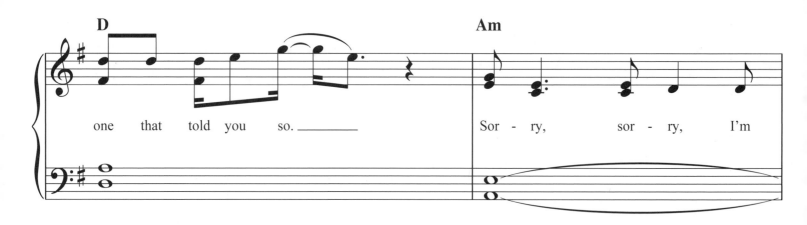

one that told you   so. _____   Sor - ry,   sor - ry,   I'm

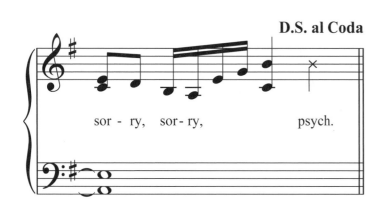

sor - ry, sor - ry,   psych.

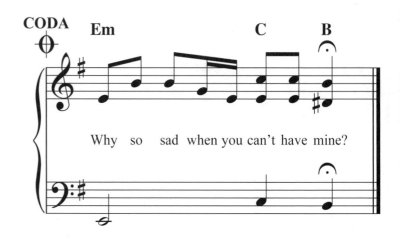

CODA   Em   C   B

Why so   sad when you can't have mine?

idontwannabeyouanymore

Words and Music by BILLIE EILISH O'CONNELL
and FINNEAS O'CONNELL

Slowly, in 2

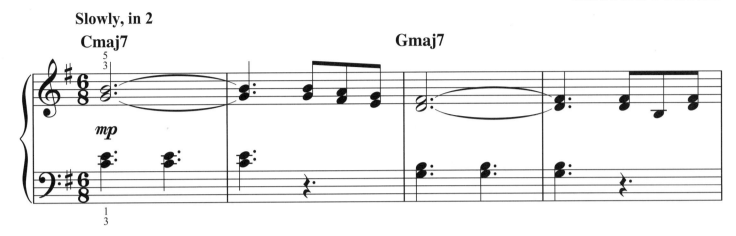

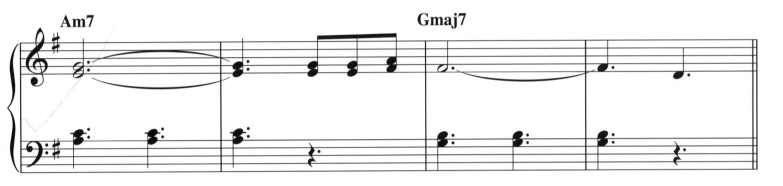

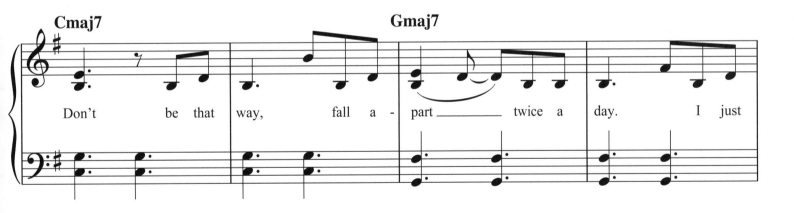

Don't be that way, fall a - part _____ twice a day. I just

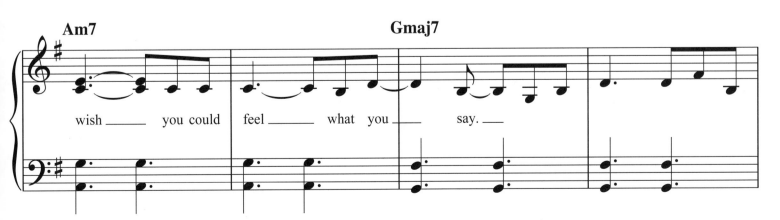

wish _____ you could feel _____ what you _____ say. _____

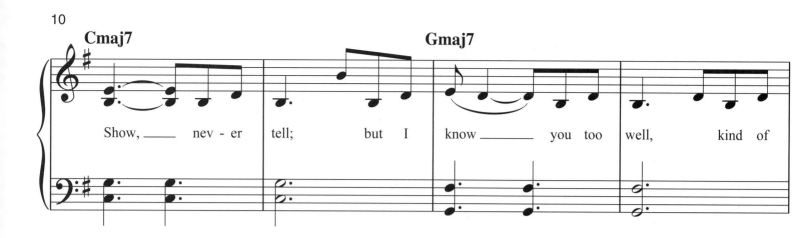

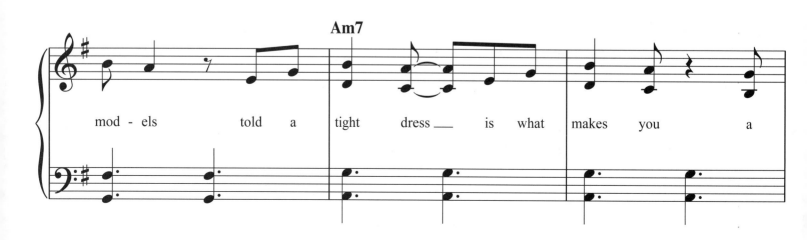

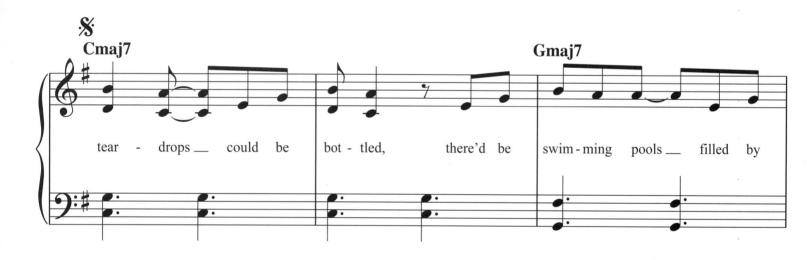

whore.　　　If "I love you" was a prom-ise, would you

break it ____ if you're hon-est, tell the mir-ror what you

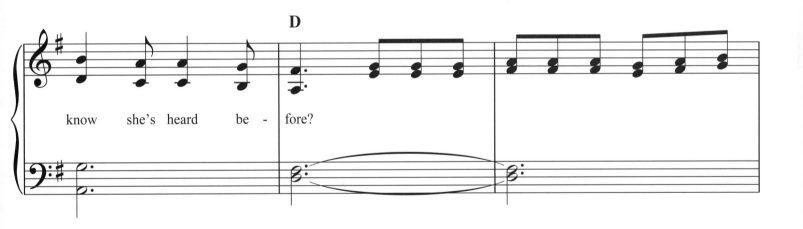

know she's heard be-fore?

To Coda ⊕

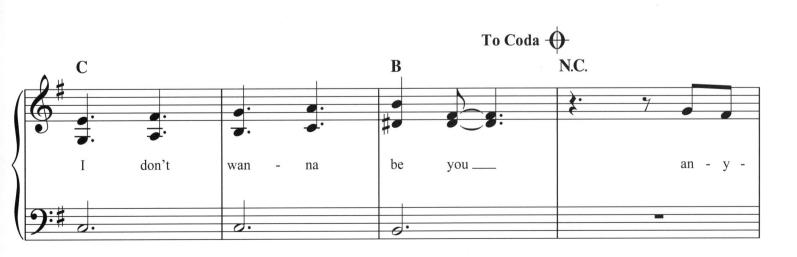

I don't wan-na be you ____ an-y-

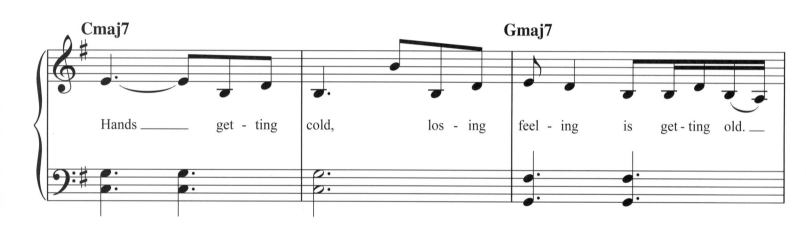

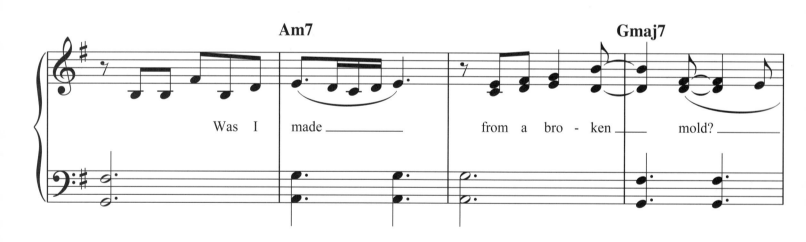

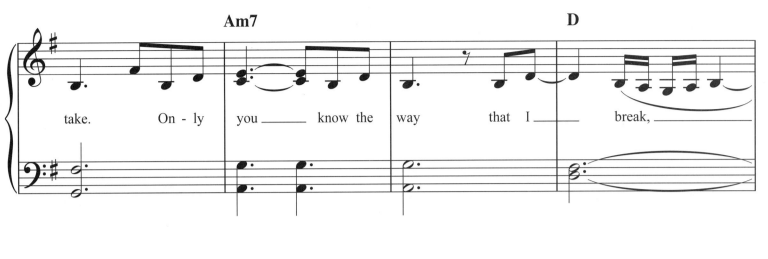

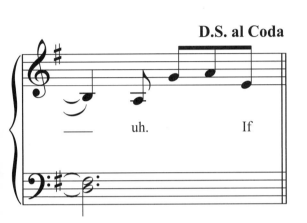

MY BOY

Words and Music by BILLIE EILISH
and FINNEAS O'CONNELL

Moderately slow

Bah, boo dah. _____ Ba, boo, dah, boo, dah, _____ mmm. _____

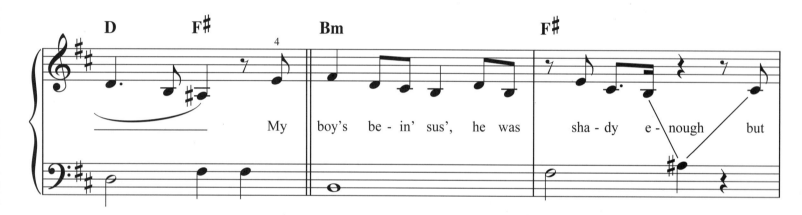

_____ My boy's be-in' sus', he was sha-dy e-nough but

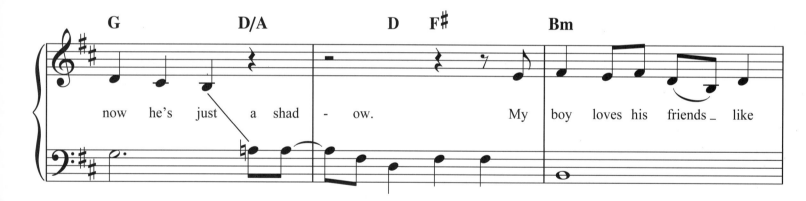

now he's just a shad - ow. My boy loves his friends _ like

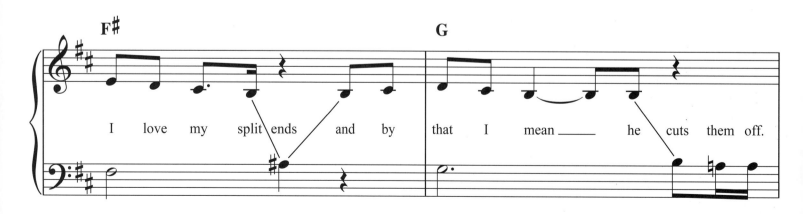

I love my split ends and by that I mean _____ he cuts them off.

Faster groove

What? My boy, my boy, my boy ____ don't

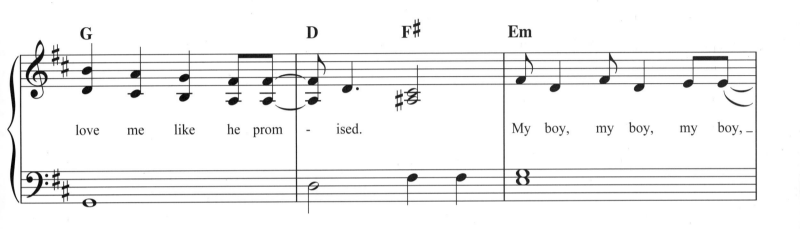

love me like he prom - ised. My boy, my boy, my boy, ___

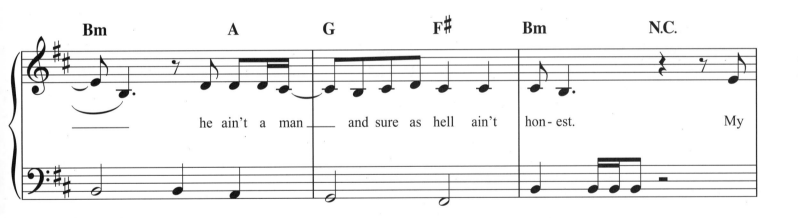

___ he ain't a man ___ and sure as hell ain't hon - est. My

boy's be - in' sus' and he don't know how to cuss. He just

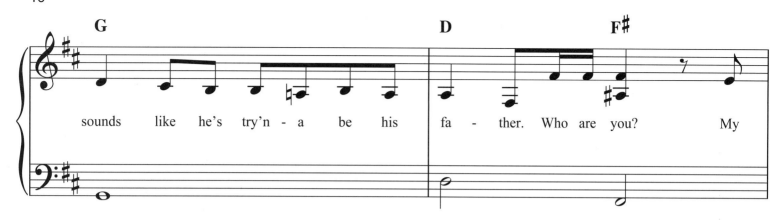

sounds like he's try'n - a be his fa - ther. Who are you? My

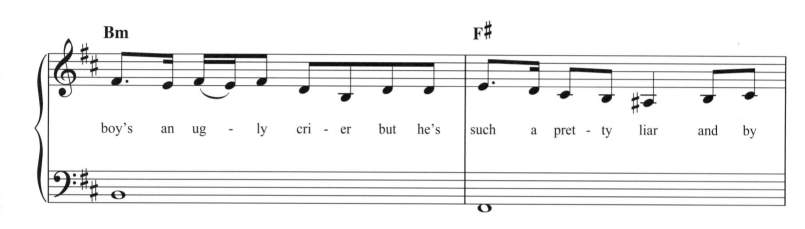

boy's an ug - ly cri - er but he's such a pret - ty liar and by

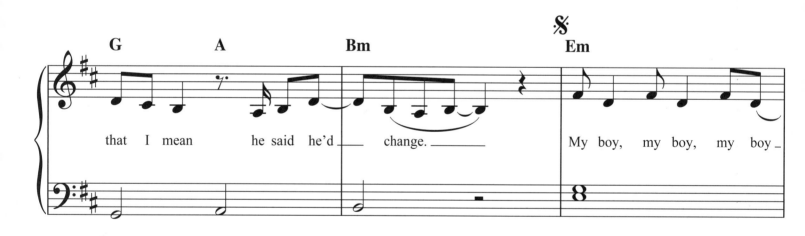

that I mean he said he'd change. My boy, my boy, my boy

don't love me like he prom - ised.

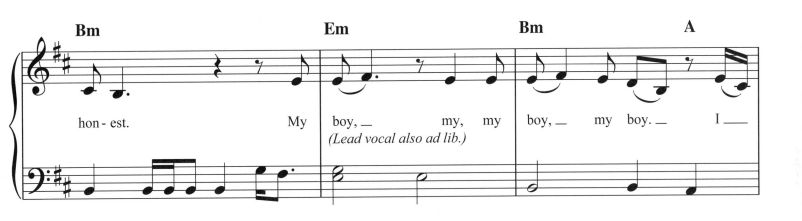

CODA

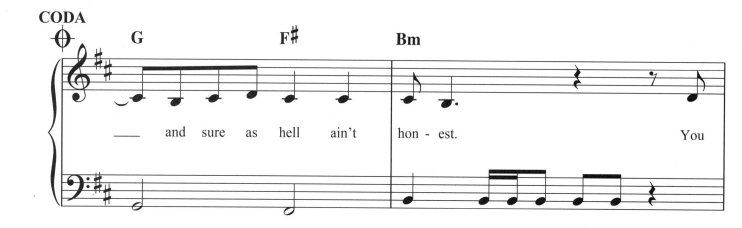

_____ and sure as hell ain't hon - est. You

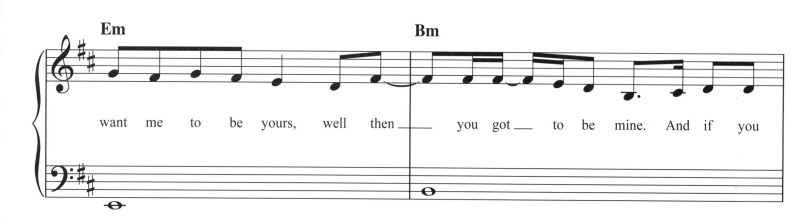

want me to be yours, well then ____ you got ____ to be mine. And if you

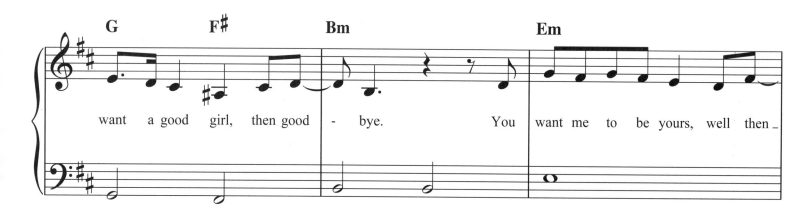

want a good girl, then good - bye. You want me to be yours, well then _

_____ you've got - ta be mine. And if you want a good girl, then good - bye.

PARTY FAVOR

Words and Music by BILLIE EILISH
and FINNEAS O'CONNELL

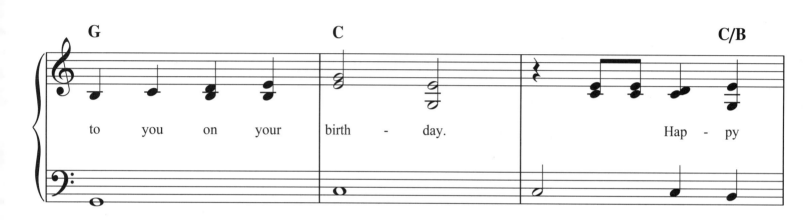

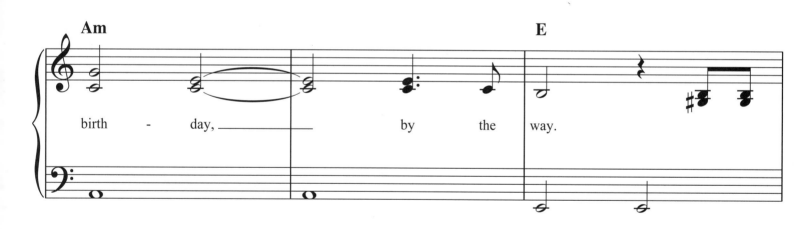

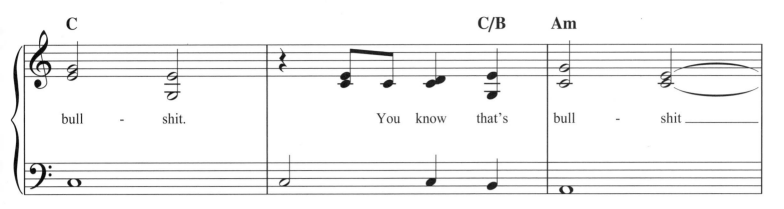

bull - shit.   You know   that's   bull - shit _____

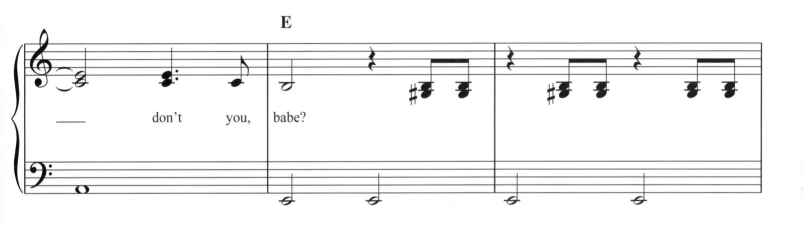

_____   don't   you,   babe?

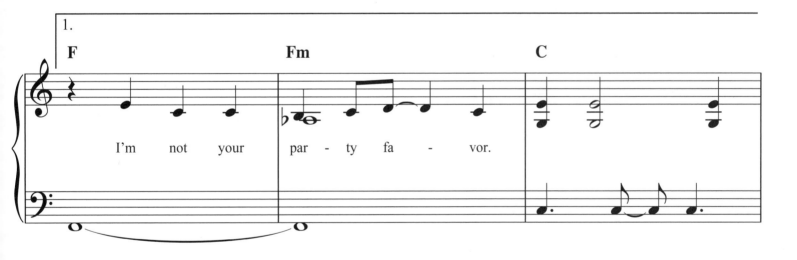

I'm   not   your   par - ty   fa - vor.

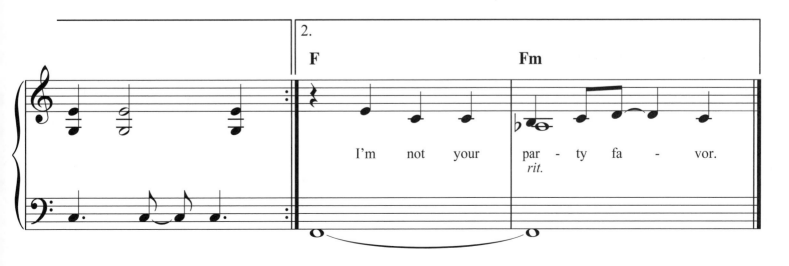

I'm   not   your   par - ty   fa - vor.
rit.

WATCH

Words and Music by
FINNEAS O'CONNELL

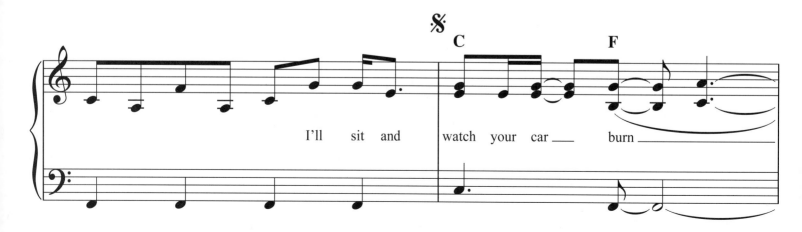

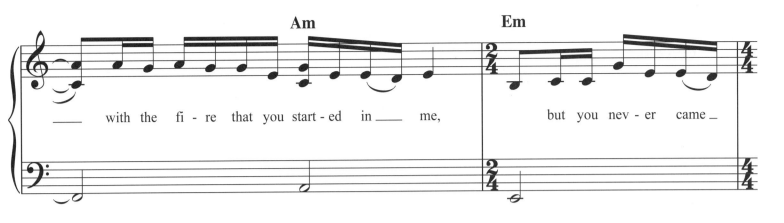

with the fi-re that you start-ed in ____ me, but you nev-er came ____

back to ask it out. ____ Go a-head and watch my heart ____ burn ____

with the fi-re that you start-ed in ____ me, but I'll nev-er let you

To Coda

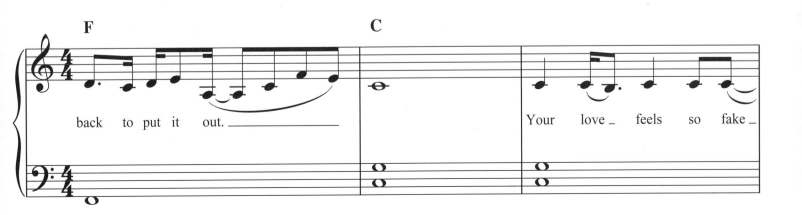

back to put it out. ____ Your love ____ feels so fake ____

and my de - mands ___ aren't _ high to ___ make. _

___ If I could get to sleep, _ I would have

slept by now. Your lies will nev - er keep, _ I think you need to

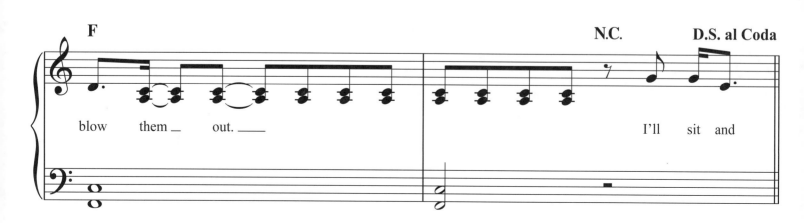

blow them _ out. ___ I'll sit and

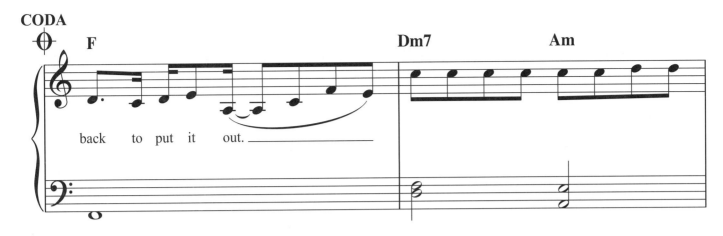

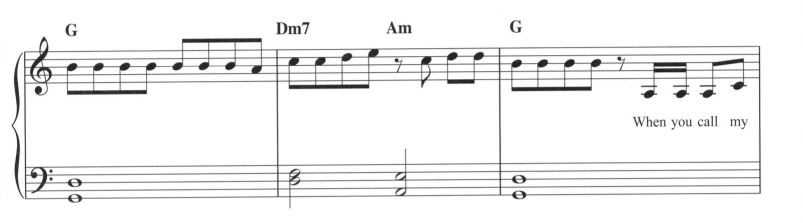

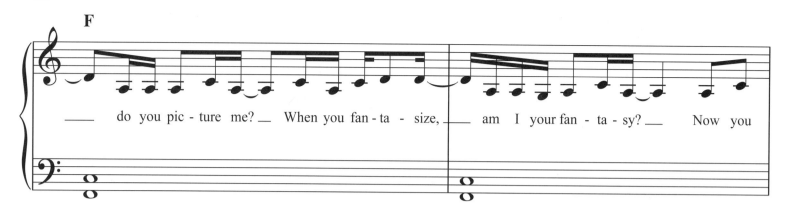

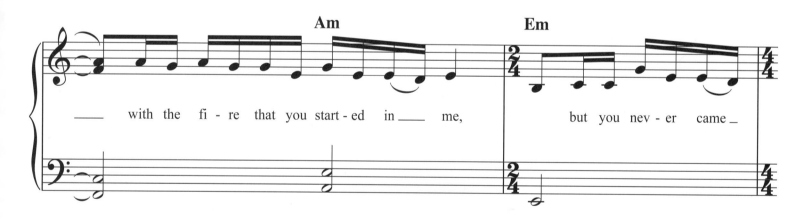

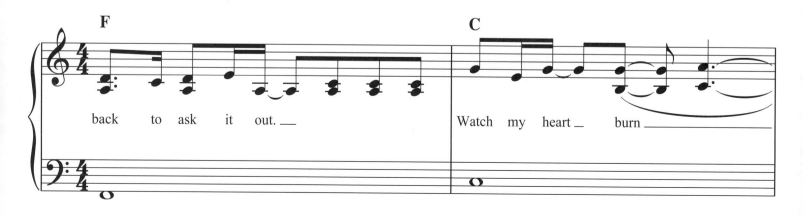

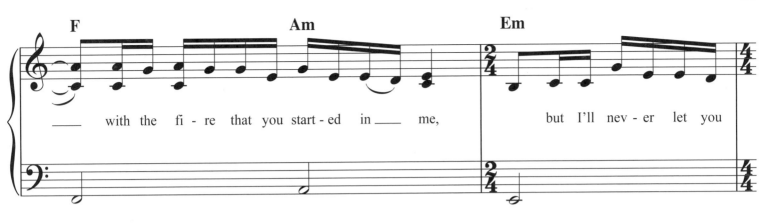

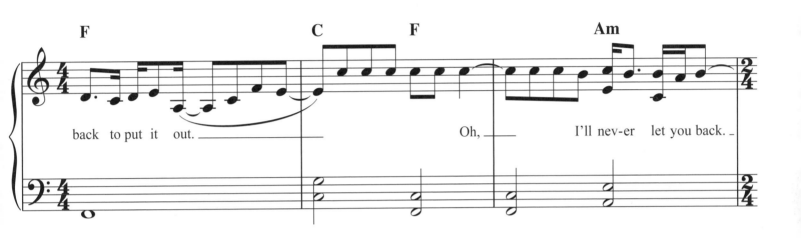

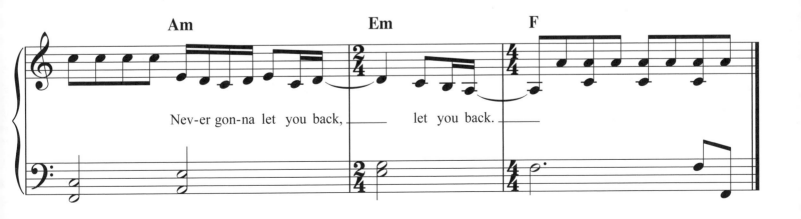

BELLYACHE

Words and Music by BILLIE EILISH
and FINNEAS O'CONNELL

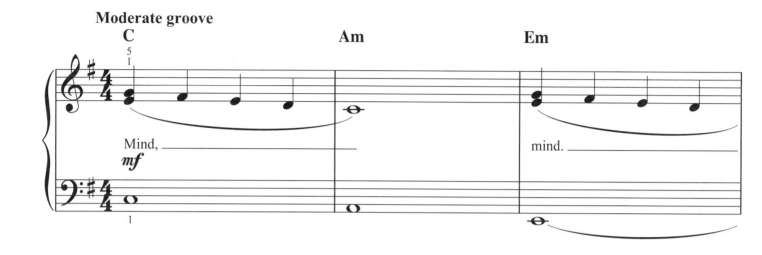

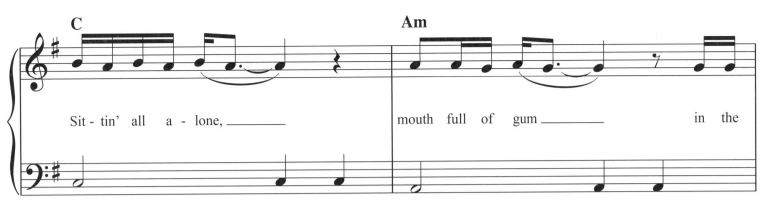

Sit - tin' all a - lone, _____ mouth full of gum _____ in the

drive - way. My

friends are - n't ___ far, _____ in the back of my car _____ lay their

bod - ies. Where's my

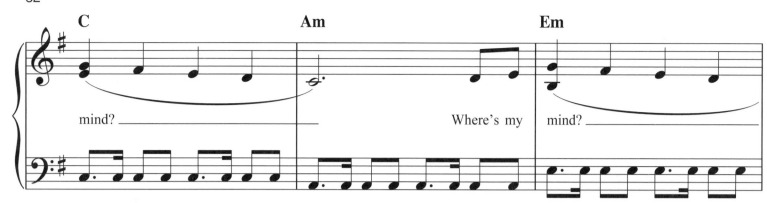

mind? _____ | Where's my | mind? _____

_____ | They'll be here pret - ty _____ soon, _____
Ev - 'ry - thing I _____ do, _____ the

look - in' through my room _____ for the mon - ey.
way I wear my noose _____ like a neck - lace.

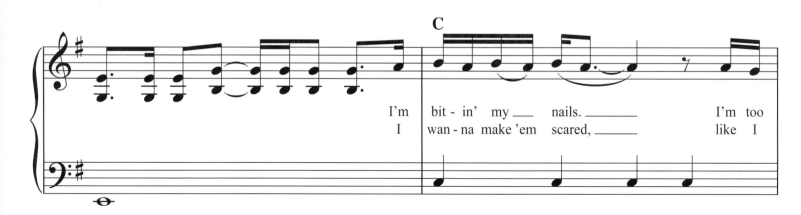

I'm bit - in' my _____ nails. _____ I'm too
I wan - na make 'em scared, _____ like I

young to go to jail, _____ it's kind - a fun - ny.
could be an - y - where, _____ like I'm reck - less.

Where's my mind? _____
I lost my mind, _____

Where's my mind? _____ Where's my
I don't mind. _____

mind? _____ Where's _ my mind? _____

Maybe it's in the gutter _____ where I _____ left my

lover. _____ What an expensive _____ fate. _____ My V is for Ven-

detta. _____ Thought that I'd _____ feel better _____ and now I've got a belly-ache.

To Coda

D.S. al Coda

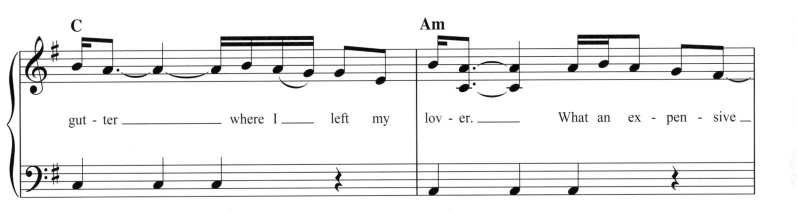

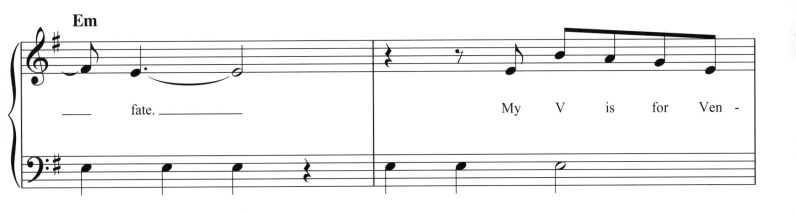

&BURN

Words and Music by FINNEAS O'CONNELL
and VINCE STAPLES

Moderately

Lips meet teeth and tongue. ___ My heart skips eight beats at once. ___
Your love feels so fake. ___ My de - mands aren't high to make. ___

___ If we were meant to be, we would have been by now.
___ If I could get to sleep, I would have slept by now. Ahh, your

See what you wan - na see, all I see is him right now. H - h -
lies will nev - er keep. I think you need to blow them out, b - b -

him right now.   I'll sit and
blow them out.   I'll sit and

watch your car ___ burn _____ with the fire _ that you

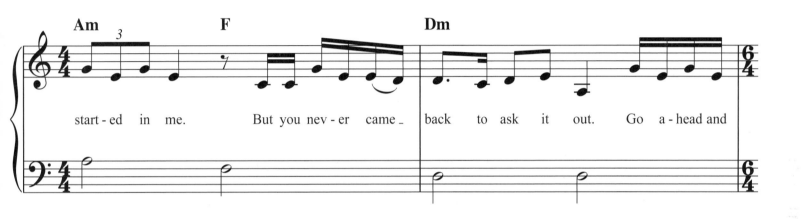

start - ed in me.   But you nev - er came _ back to ask it out.   Go a - head and

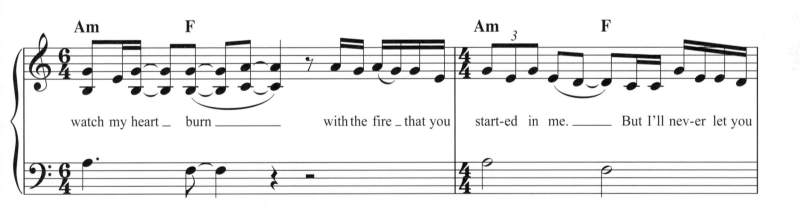

watch my heart _ burn _____ with the fire _ that you   start-ed in me. _____ But I'll nev-er let you

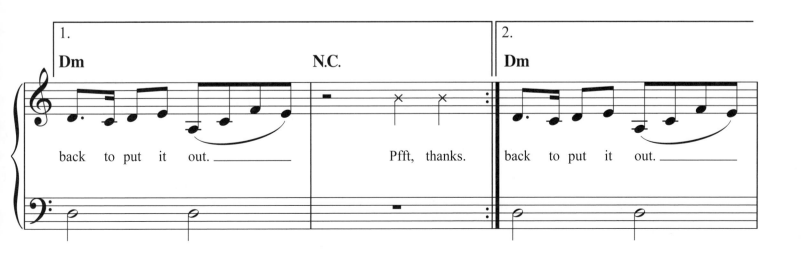

1.

back to put it out. _____   Pfft, thanks.

2.

back to put it out. _____

Oh, oh, oh, oh, _____ oh, oh, oh, oh, oh, oh. *Rap: (See additional lyrics.)*

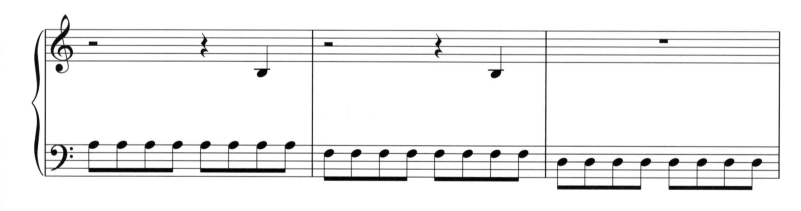

And I'll watch your car __ burn __ with the fire __ that you

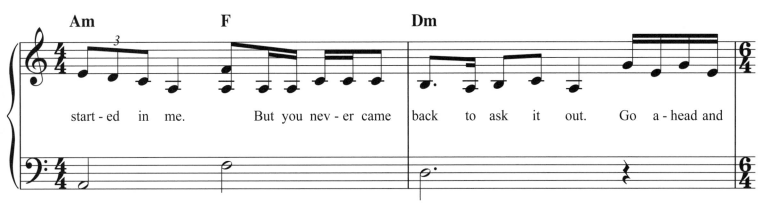

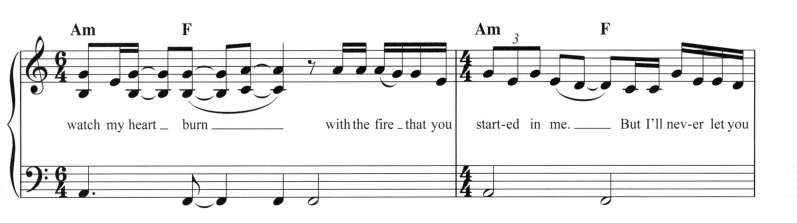

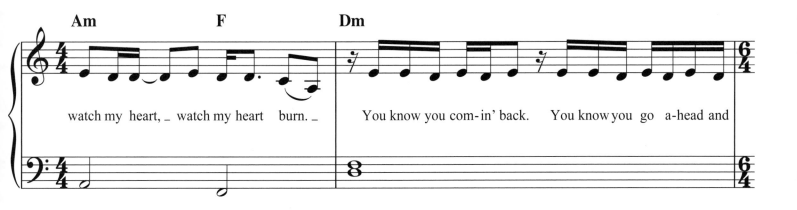

Additional Lyrics

Rap: 7-4-2008, I still remember that. Heaven sent a present my way.
I won't forget your laugh. Packin' everything when you leave.
You know you comin' back. Wanna see me down on my knees but that
was made for a ring. I try to wait for the storm to calm down but that's stubborn, baby.
Leadin' the war, we drawn down on each other. Try'n to even the score.
We all been found guilty in the court of aorta.

OCEAN EYES

Words and Music by
FINNEAS O'CONNELL

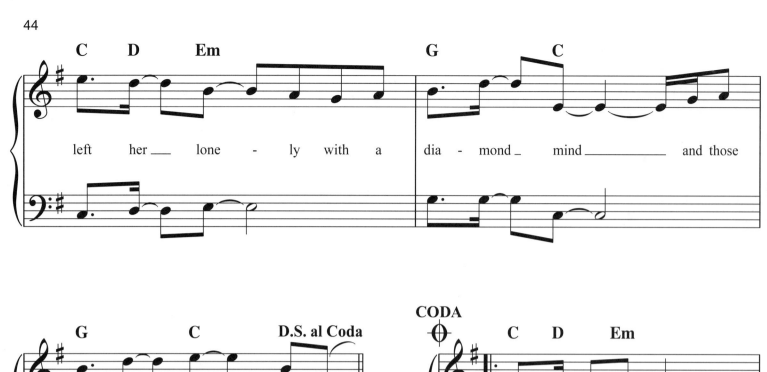

left her ___ lone - ly with a dia - mond ___ mind _____ and those

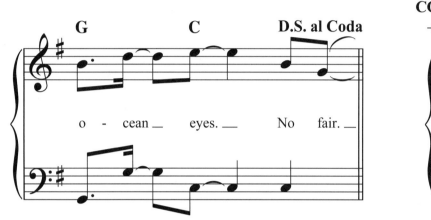

o - cean ___ eyes. ___ No fair. ___

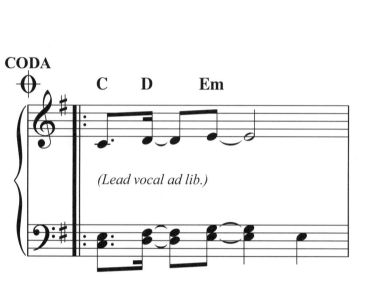

CODA

(Lead vocal ad lib.)

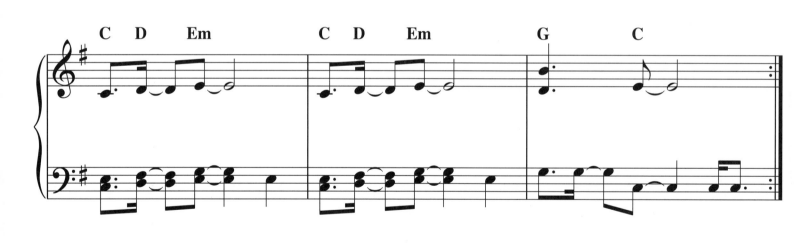

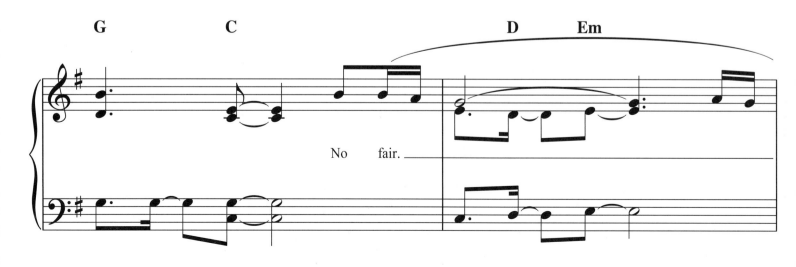

No fair. _____

HOSTAGE

Words and Music by BILLIE EILISH
and FINNEAS O'CONNELL

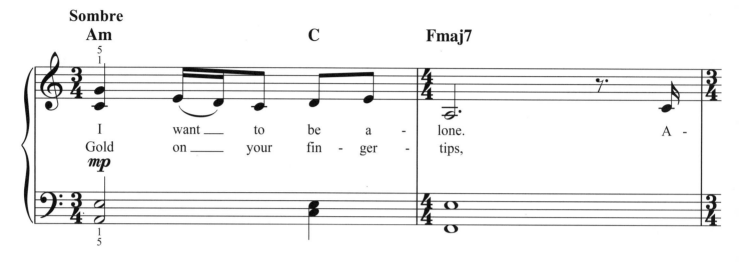

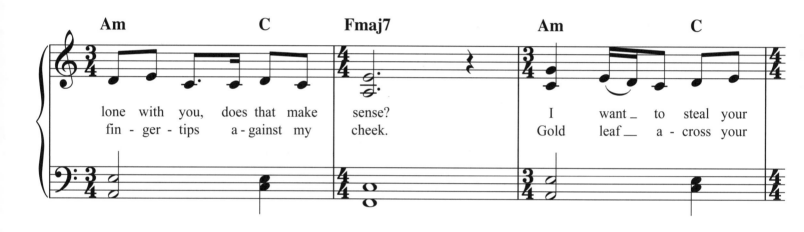

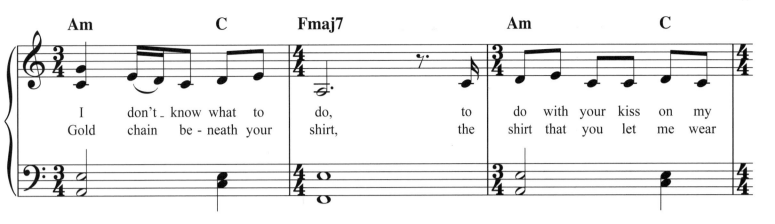

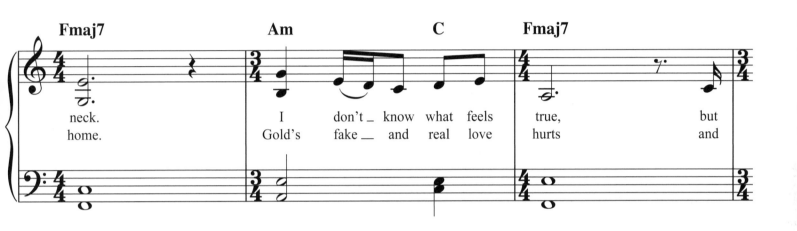

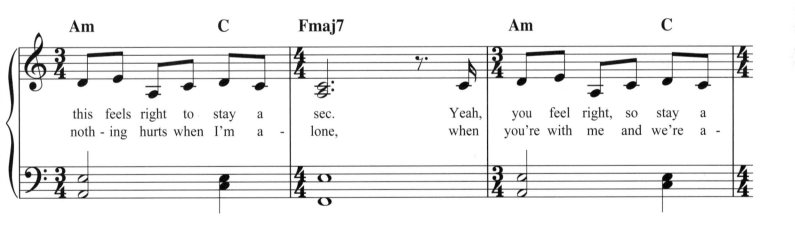

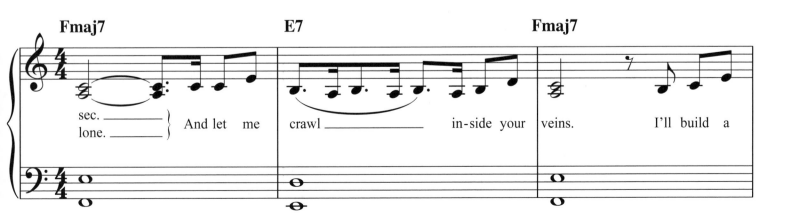

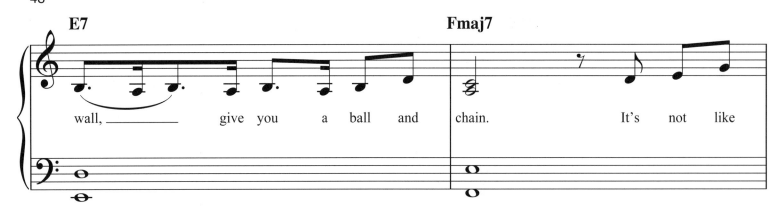

wall, _____ give you a ball and chain. It's not like

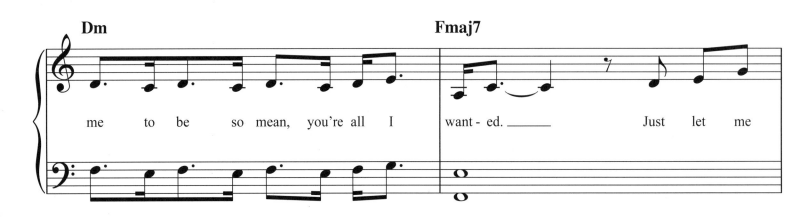

me to be so mean, you're all I want - ed. _____ Just let me

hold _____ you like a hos - tage. _

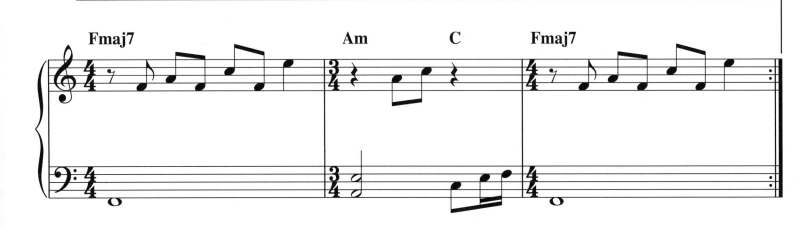

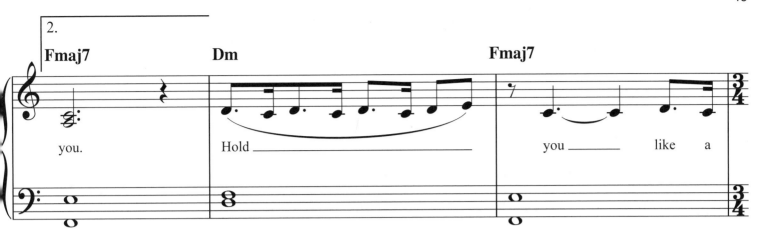

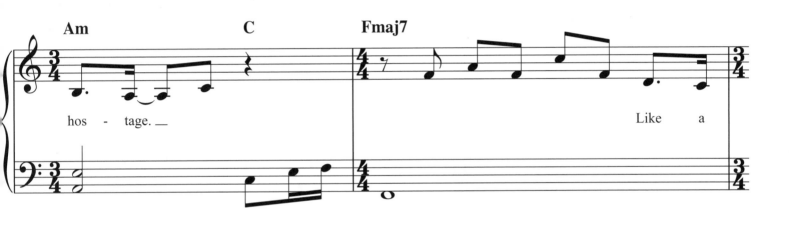

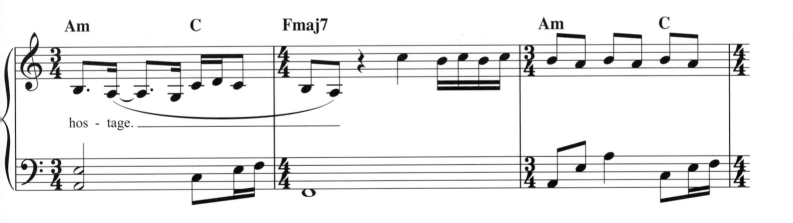

LOVELY

Words and Music by BILLIE EILISH O'CONNELL,
FINNEAS O'CONNELL and KHALID ROBINSON

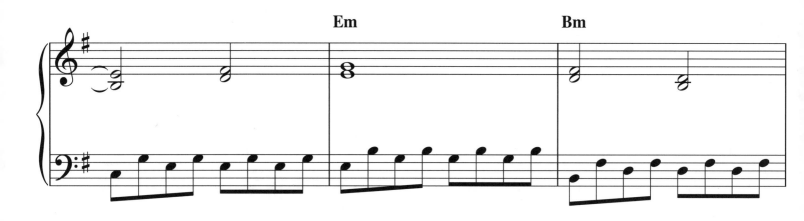

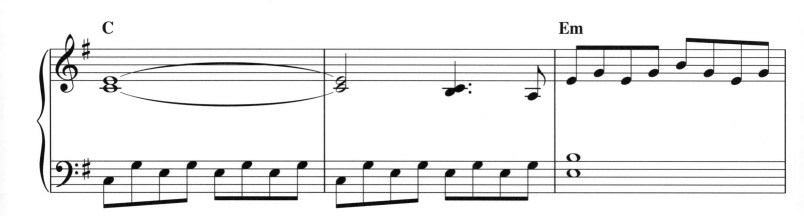

Gmaj7/B **Bm** **C**

Thought I found a way,

Em **Bm** **C**

thought I found a way out. But you nev - er go a - way,

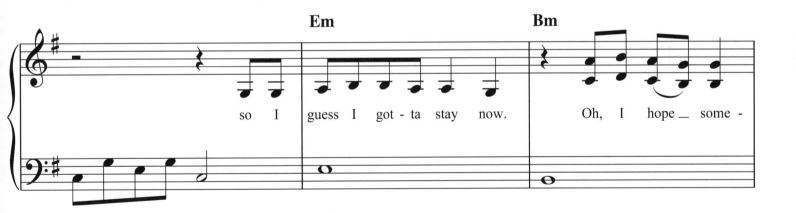

Em **Bm**

so I guess I got - ta stay now. Oh, I hope __ some -

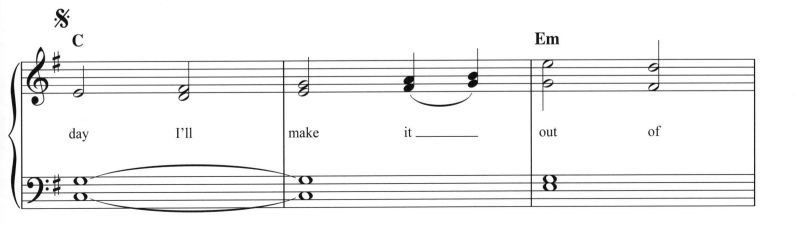

C **Em**

day I'll make it _____ out of

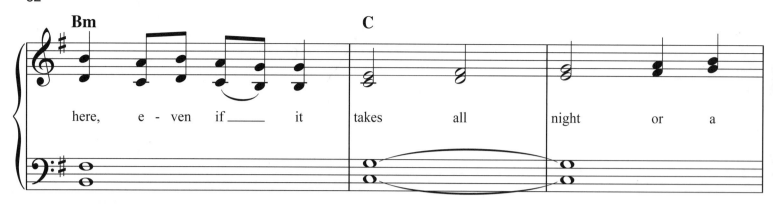

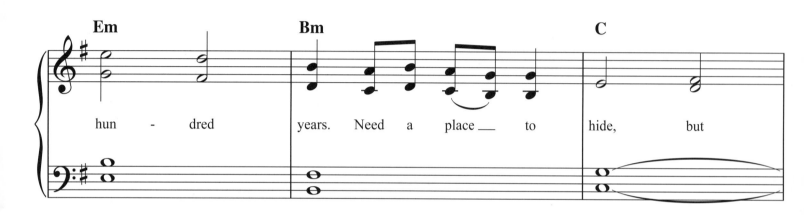

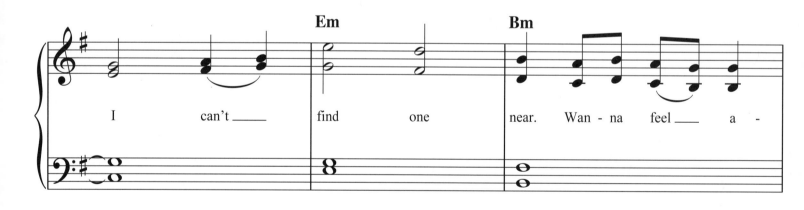

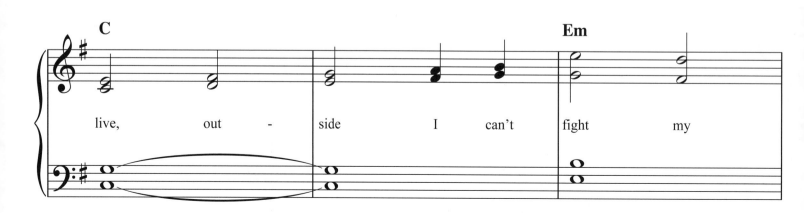

53

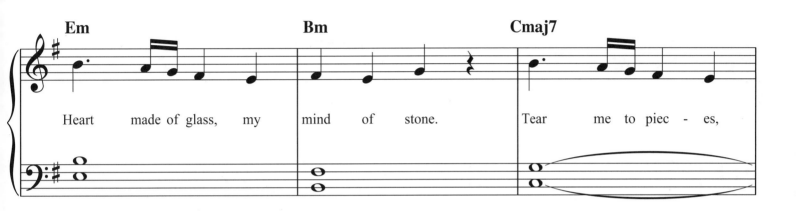

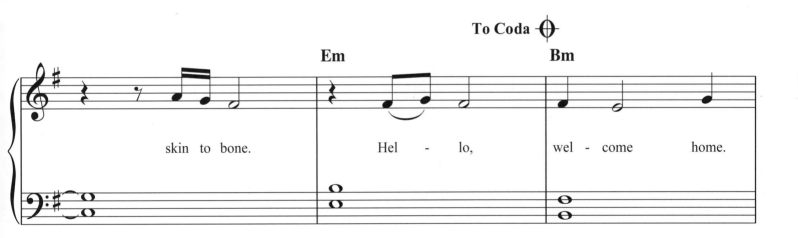

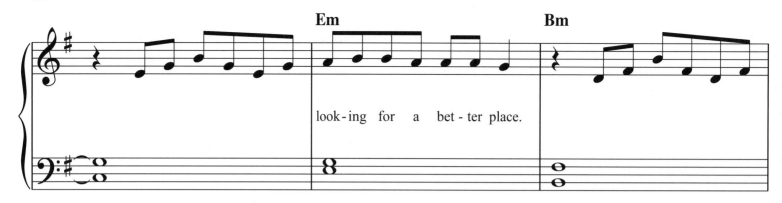

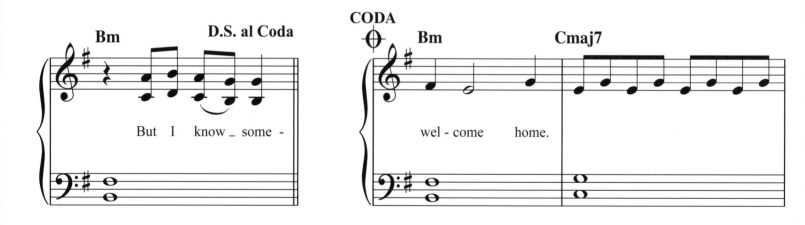

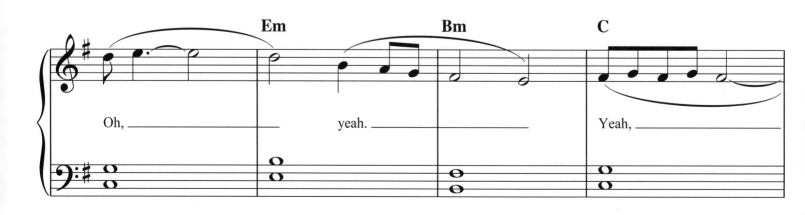

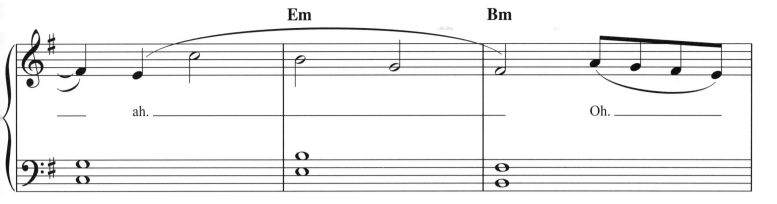

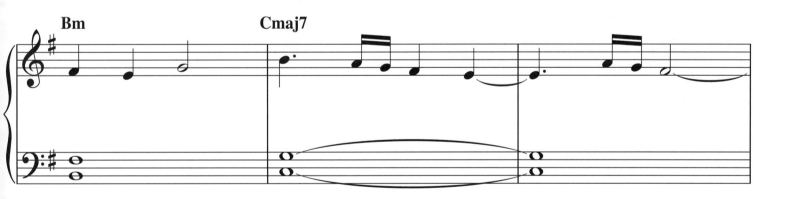

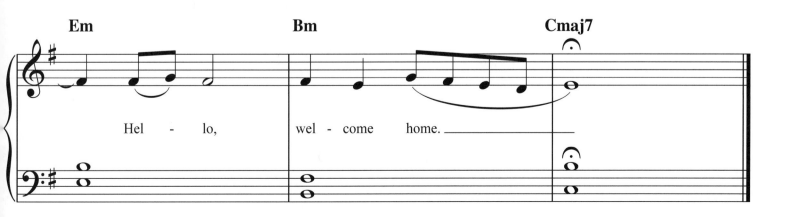